The Sandwich Challenge

Dive into Sandwich world!!
Learn how to surprise your taste at home!!

By

Erik Nielsen

The trademarks that are used are without any consent, and the publication of the trademark is without permission or backing by the trademark owner. All trademarks and brands within this book are for clarifying purposes only and are the owned by the owners themselves, not affiliated with this document.

Table of contents

ABC Sandwich

1 cup mayonnaise

1/2 cup minced scallions 2 tablespoons brandy

1/4 teaspoon coarsely-ground black pepper 18 slices toasted whole-wheat bread

Leaf lettuce

12 ounces crabmeat, picked over well to remove any shells

Tomato slices

12 slices slab bacon, cut in half, cooked crisp and drained

2 avocados, sliced

In a small bowl, combine the mayonnaise, scallion and brandy, mixing well. For each sandwich, spread three pieces of bread with a portion of the mayonnaise mixture. Cover the first slice of bread with lettuce leaves, 2 ounces of crabmeat, and one or two tomato slices. Add the second slice of bread, and top with the four half-slices of bacon, a layer of avocado slices, another tomato slice or two, and more lettuce. Cover with the third slice of bread, secure the sandwich with wooden picks, if you like, and slice it in half.

Serve the sandwiches immediately.

Acapulco Fishburgers

1 pound fish fillets

medium green bell pepper, chopped 3 medium onions, chopped

cups soft bread crumbs 3/4 teaspoon salt

1/4 teaspoon pepper

tablespoons shortening

Bone fish; put through food chopper or chop finely with knife. Combine with green pepper, onions, bread crumbs, salt and pepper; mix well. Shape into 8 patties about 4 inches in diameter. Brown on both sides in shortening in skillet over moderate heat for 10 to 15 minutes.

Alaska Salmon Salad Sandwich

15 1/2 ounces canned Alaska salmon 1/3 cup plain nonfat yogurt

1/3 cup chopped green onions 1/3 cup chopped celery

1 tablespoon lemon juice Black pepper, to taste 12 slices bread

Drain and flake salmon. Stir in remaining ingredients except pepper and bread. Season with pepper to taste. Spread salmon mixture on half of bread slices; top with remaining bread. Cut sandwiches into halves or quarters.

Makes 6 sandwiches.

Asian Turkey Burgers

1 pound ground turkey

1 1/3 cups canned French fried onions, divided 1 egg

1/2 cup finely chopped water chestnuts 1/4 cup dry breadcrumbs

3 tablespoons teriyaki sauce

1 tablespoon Frank's RedHot sauce 2 teaspoons grated fresh ginger

4 sandwich buns Shredded lettuce

Combine turkey, 1 cup French fried onions, egg, water chestnuts, breadcrumbs, teriyaki sauce, hot sauce and ginger. Shape into 4 patties. Broil about 6 inches from heat or grill over medium heat 10 minutes or until no longer pink in center, turning once.

Serve on buns, topped with remaining 1/3 cup French fried onions and lettuce. Yield: 4 burgers

Avocado and Chicken Tortas

fully ripened Mexican avocado

(6-inch) sandwich rolls (such as Portuguese or submarine rolls), halved Salt and freshly ground black pepper, to taste

8 ounces grilled chicken breast, sliced

1 cup shredded iceberg or romaine lettuce 1 tomato, sliced

2/3 cup mashed black beans, divided 1/4 cup pickled jalapeño pepper slices

Cut lengthwise around middle of avocado; twist avocado to separate halves; strike pit with a knife blade to remove; scoop out pulp with a spoon.

In a small bowl, mash avocado.

To assemble tortas: Spread mashed avocado on cut sides of rolls, dividing evenly. Sprinkle with salt and pepper. On bottom halves, layer sliced chicken, lettuce, tomato, black beans and jalapeño pepper slices. Firmly press tops of rolls on tortas.

Yield: 2 sandwiches

Avocado Bacon Sandwiches

1/4 pound bacon slices, chopped 1 ripe avocado

1/2 teaspoon lemon juice Salt and pepper, to taste

tablespoons butter, softened

large slices whole wheat bread

Lemon twist and parsley sprig, to garnish Fry bacon until crisp. Drain on paper towels.

Peel avocado, taking care not to remove bright green flesh just inside the skin. Cut in half and remove seed. In a bowl, mash avocado, then stir in lemon juice, salt and pepper.

Butter two slices of bread. Spread avocado mixture on buttered sides of 2 bread slices. Scatter bacon over avocado. Cover with remaining bread slices, buttered sides down, and press together.

Cut off bread crusts. Cut each sandwich into 4 triangles. Arrange on a serving plate, garnished with a lemon twist and parsley sprig.

Avocado Chicken Melt

4 boneless skinless chicken breast halves 1/2 cup cornmeal

teaspoon garlic salt

tablespoons vegetable oil

1/2 firm ripe avocado, peeled and sliced thin, divided 1 cup shredded Monterey jack cheese

4 wheat bread slices, toasted 1/2 cup plain yogurt

1/4 cup chopped sweet red bell pepper

Rinse chicken with cold water and pat dry with paper towels. Place between two sheets of plastic wrap and pound to flatten to 1/4-inch thickness.

In resealable plastic bag, combine cornmeal and garlic salt. Add chicken; close bag and toss to coat well. In large nonstick frying pan, heat oil. Cook chicken in hot oil for 2 minutes per side or until lightly browned. Remove chicken from pan and place in shallow baking pan.

Place half of avocado slices over chicken and sprinkle evenly with shredded cheese. Bake at 350 degrees F for 15 minutes or until chicken is done and cheese is melted.

Place each chicken breast on a slice of toast. Top with remaining avocado slices. In small bowl, combine yogurt and pepper; serve with chicken.

Yields 4 servings.

Avocado Monte Cristo

A signature sandwich served west-coast style. Fresh avocados layered with turkey, Jalapeno Jack cheese, cilantro and salsa.

Serves 12

3/4 cup garlic mayonnaise (aioli) 24 slices firm white sandwich bread 6 California avocados (3 pound)

48 (1 ounce) slices sliced roasted chicken or turkey (3 pound) 24 (1 ounce) slices sliced Jalapeno Jack cheese

16 eggs, beaten

1 teaspoon salt

Unsalted butter, as needed

3 cups fresh fruit salsa of choice 12 fresh cilantro sprigs

Spread 1/2 tablespoon garlic mayonnaise on one side of each slice of bread. Cover 12 slices of bread with avocado slices. Top each with 2 slices of chicken or turkey and 1 slice cheese. Cover each with remaining slice of bread, spread-side down, diagonally cut each in half. Reserve.

Beat together egg, milk, and salt; reserve. Dip 2 halves of a sandwich in egg mixture, coating well. Brown in hot butter, about 2 minutes per side.

Serve with 1/4 cup fresh fruit salsa. Garnish with a cilantro sprig.

Avocado Quesadillas

2 ripe tomatoes, seeded and diced

firm-ripe Haas avocado, peeled and diced 1 tablespoon chopped red onion

teaspoons fresh lemon juice 1/4 teaspoon Tabasco sauce 1/4 cup sour cream

tablespoons chopped fresh cilantro 4 (6- to 7-inch) flour tortillas

1/2 teaspoon vegetable oil

1/3 cups coarsely grated Monterey jack cheese Fresh cilantro sprigs (for garnish)

In a small bowl stir together tomatoes, avocado, onion, lemon juice and Tabasco sauce. Season with salt and pepper.

In another small bowl stir together sour cream and cilantro and salt and pepper to taste.

Preheat broiler. Put tortillas on a large baking sheet and brush tops with oil. Broil tortillas on a rack set 2 to 4 inches from heat until pale golden. Turn tortillas and broil until other sides are pale golden. Sprinkle tortillas evenly with cheese and broil until cheese is melted and bubbling. Spread avocado mixture evenly over tortillas and top each with 1 of remaining tortillas, cheese side down, to make 2 quesadillas. Transfer quesadillas to a cutting board and cut each into 4 wedges.

Top each wedge with a heaping teaspoon of sour cream mixture and garnish with cilantro sprigs.

Baked Beer Burgers

pounds ground beef Pepper

1 tablespoon Tabasco sauce 1 garlic clove, crushed

1/3 cup chili sauce

1/2 envelope dry onion soup mix 1/2 cup beer, divided

Preheat oven to 400°F.

Combine meat, pepper, Tabasco sauce, garlic, chili sauce, dry onion soup mix and 1/4 cup of the beer. Shape into 6 patties. Bake at 400 degrees F until brown, about 10 minutes. Baste

Baked Cheese Sandwiches

12 slices bread

6 slices American cheese Butter

4 eggs

1 1/2 cups milk

Cut off crusts and spread bread with butter. Place cheese between 2 slices. Place sandwiches side by side in a 13 x 9-inch baking dish. Beat eggs with milk. Pour over sandwiches and let stand for 1 hour or overnight. Bake 1/2 hour at 350 degrees F.

Serve with cream of mushroom soup slightly diluted with milk poured over the top and warmed

Baked Crabmeat Sandwich

12 slices thin bread, trimmed and buttered

1 cup (7 1/2 ounces) crabmeat

4 eggs, beaten 1/2 teaspoon salt

1/2 pound cheese, grated 3 cups milk

1/2 teaspoon curry powder

Place six slices bread, butter side up, in casserole. Spread crabmeat over; add 6 more slices bread, butter side up. Sprinkle with grated cheese. Mix eggs, seasonings and milk together and pour carefully over bread. Cover and place in refrigerator several hours or overnight. Bake 45 minutes at 325 degrees F.

Serves 8 to 10.

Barbecue Burgers

1/2 cup onion, chopped 2 tablespoons flour

1 tablespoon prepared mustard 1/4 teaspoon pepper

1 pound ground beef 6 tablespoons catsup 1/2 teaspoon salt

1 cup sour cream 8 hamburger buns

Brown onion and beef. Add flour, catsup, mustard, salt and pepper. Add sour cream. Serve on lightly-toasted hamburger buns.

Barbecue Frankburgers

1 pound hot dogs

1 1/2 tablespoons Worcestershire sauce 1/4 cup vinegar

1 to 2 tablespoons granulated sugar 1/2 cup catsup

1/2 cup water

1/2 cup chopped onions

1/2 cup chopped green bell pepper Hot dog buns

In an oblong glass dish, place hot dogs.

Combine remaining ingredients except buns. Pour over hot dogs and bake at 350 degrees F for 1 hour.

Serve in hot dog buns. Variation

Use ground beef patties in place of hot dogs and serve on hamburger buns.

Barbecue Pork on Buns

1 (2-pound) boneless pork loin 1 onion, chopped

3/4 cup cola carbonated beverage 3/4 cup barbecue sauce

8 sandwich buns

Combine all ingredients except buns in a 4-quart crockpot; cook, covered, on HIGH for 5 to 6 hours, until very tender. Drain and slice or shred pork; serve on buns with additional barbecue sauce, if desired.

Serves 8.

Tip: Pork can be made 1 to 2 days ahead; refrigerate covered and reheat before serving.

Barbecue Quesadillas

8 (10-inch) flour tortillas

12 ounces smoked or barbecued meat 2 cups shredded Cheddar cheese

1 cup sautéed red bell peppers, julienne 1 cup sautéed onions, julienne

1 cup sautéed sliced mushrooms Barbecue sauce

Sauté onions, peppers and mushrooms and place in bowl. Shred or chop your meat and coat lightly with barbecue sauce.

Preheat nonstick skillet on medium. Spray pan with Pam. Place on tortilla in pan and cover entire tortilla with layer of cheese. Top cheese with smoked sauced meat and sautéed vegetables.

Cover everything with another tortilla. Spray top of second tortilla with Pam and turn over after the bottom is browned. When the bottom of the second tortilla is browned, remove from pan and cut into wedges. Repeat process until all tortillas are used.

Serve on a large platter with salsa, sour cream and guacamole.

Barbecued Brisket

1 (4 to 5 pound) fresh beef brisket

(5 ounce) bottle Liquid Smoke 3 teaspoons garlic salt

teaspoons onion salt 2 teaspoons celery salt

1 (18 ounce) bottle barbecue sauce Heavy-duty aluminum foil

Line a 12 x 9-inch or larger baking dish with heavy-duty aluminum foil, allowing enough foil to cover meat. Turn brisket fat-side down and pour entire bottle of Liquid Smoke over meat. Sprinkle the 3 salts over meat. Turn brisket over (fat side on top) and seal with foil. Marinate overnight.

Next morning pour off marinade; bake in a 225 degree F oven for 5 hours. Let cool.

Pour off gravy and refrigerate until cold. Slice meat with meat slicer on a thin setting or use an electric knife. Layer in casserole dish the brisket and barbecue sauce; repeat several times. Cook an additional 30 to 45 minutes in a 300 degree F oven until warm.

Yields 8 to 10 servings.

Barbecued Pork and Beef Sandwiches

In a crockpot, combine the following:

1/2 pounds lean stew beef 1 1/2 pounds lean pork cubes 1 cup finely chopped onion

cups finely chopped green bell pepper Combine the following ingredients:

1 (6 ounce) can tomato paste 1/2 cup brown sugar

1/4 cup cider vinegar

tablespoon chili powder 1 teaspoon salt

teaspoon Worcestershire sauce 1 teaspoon dry mustard

Blend all of these ingredients well and add to the crockpot. Stir into the meat, onion and pepper mixture. Cover and cook on HIGH for 8 hours. Stir to shred meat before serving on buttered rolls or pita bread.

NOTE: If you do not have a crockpot, you can simmer this mixture on top of the stove. Use a very heavy Dutch oven with a tight-fitting lid.

This may also be served over rice rather than using rolls, if desired. Leftovers freeze great.

Barbecued Pork Sandwiches

pork roast

cups catsup

1 cup vinegar

3 tablespoons Worcestershire sauce 1 tablespoon prepared mustard

1/2 tablespoon Tabasco sauce (or to taste) 4 tablespoons butter

1/2 cup brown sugar Buns

in stockpot, boil meat in water for 4 hours or until it is falling apart. Of course one can always use leftover pork roast but you will need a lot!!

Remove meat, cool, shred. Discard the liquid. In same pot, add catsup, vinegar, Worcestershire sauce, mustard, Tabasco, butter and brown sugar. Boil for 5 minutes, stirring. Mix in the shredded pork and simmer for at least 30 minutes but longer is even better!!

Barbecued Slaw Burgers

2 pounds ground beef 1 medium onion, diced

1 bottle barbecue sauce 1 sauce bottle water

5 to 6 tablespoons brown sugar Buns

Cole slaw

Brown ground beef and onion in small amount of hot shortening. Add barbecue sauce, water and brown sugar. Bring to boil; simmer for 2 hours.

Serve on buns with cole slaw. Yields 10 to 12 servings.

Barbecued Turkey on Focaccia

4 pieces focaccia or thick-sliced, country-style rosemary bread

1/2 ripe avocado, mashed

1 teaspoon fresh lemon juice

1/4 teaspoon prepared horseradish 8 slices barbecued turkey breast

4 slices canned pineapple, drained 4 teaspoons honey mustard

1/4 cup shredded Swiss cheese Lightly toast bread.

In small bowl combine avocado, lemon juice and horseradish. Divide into four portions and spread on bread. Top each sandwich with two slices of turkey and a pineapple slice. Spread 1 teaspoon mustard over each sandwich; sprinkle 1 tablespoon cheese over each and place under broiler, cooking until cheese is melted and lightly browned.

Serve warm.

BBQ Pork Sandwiches

Prepare slaw; let stand to allow flavors to blend. Make molasses marinade for pork, then broil. Serves: 6 - Work Time: 10 minutes - Total Time: 25 to 30 minutes

3 tablespoons light molasses 3 tablespoons catsup

1 tablespoon Worcestershire sauce

1 teaspoon minced, peeled fresh ginger 1/2 teaspoon grated lemon peel

garlic clove, crushed with garlic press

whole pork tenderloins (3/4 pound each) 12 small, soft dinner rolls

Preheat broiler if manufacturer directs. In medium bowl, combine molasses, catsup, Worcestershire, ginger, lemon peel, and garlic, add pork, turning to coat.

Place pork on rack in broiling pan. Spoon any remaining molasses mixture over pork tenderloins. With broiling pan 5 to 7 inches from source of heat, broil pork 15 to 20 minutes, turning pork once, until meat is browned on the outside and still slightly pink in the center (internal temperature of tenderloins should be 160 degrees F on meat thermometer).

To serve, thinly slice pork. Serve on dinner rolls with any juices from broiling pan.

Beef Burgers

pound ground beef 3 teaspoons catsup

teaspoons mustard

1 small onion, chopped 1 teaspoon salt

1/2 cup bread, broken into small pieces 1/4 cup milk

1 1/2 teaspoons Worcestershire sauce

Mix all ingredients together. Broil in oven, or grill.

Beef Sandwiches

tablespoon dried minced onion 2 teaspoons salt

teaspoons garlic powder 2 teaspoons dried oregano

1 teaspoon dried rosemary, crushed 1 teaspoon caraway seeds

1 teaspoon dried marjoram 1 teaspoon celery seed

1/4 teaspoon cayenne pepper

1 (4 to 4 1/2 pound) boneless chuck roast, halved 8 to 10 sandwich rolls, split

Combine seasonings; rub over roast. Place in a crockpot. Cover and cook on LOW for 6 to 8 hours or until meat is tender. Shred with a fork.

Serve on rolls.

NOTE: No liquid is added to the crockpot because the moisture comes from the roast.

Beef Sandwiches with Onion Marmalade

Serves 4.

3/4 pound thinly sliced deli roast beef 1 cup white or yellow onion, chopped 1 cup purple onion, chopped

3 green onions, chopped 2 tablespoons oil

1/4 cup granulated sugar

2 tablespoons cider vinegar

1 teaspoon Worcestershire sauce 1/4 teaspoon salt

1/8 teaspoon pepper Dash ground gloves

4 French rolls (6-inches) 4 endive or lettuce leaves

To make Onion Marmalade, sauté onions in oil in a large saucepan over medium-low heat 1 hour or until very tender, stirring occasionally. Stir in sugar, vinegar, Worcestershire, salt, pepper, and ground cloves. Cook over low heat, stirring occasionally 25-30 minutes or until liquid evaporates. Cool completely.

Refrigerate in a tightly covered container up to 1 week.

To assemble sandwiches, bring onion mixture to room temperature. Place endive or lettuce leaves on bottom halves of toasted rolls. Arrange beef over endive. Spread onion mixture evenly over beef. Place top halves on rolls. Cut each sandwich in half.

Benedictine

2 cucumbers, peeled

1 medium onion

pound cream cheese

to 3 drops green food coloring

Grate cucumber and onion (may use food processor) and drain well in a strainer, pressing down with spoon to remove all liquid. Discard liquid. Add drained cucumbers and onion to cream cheese and mix well in food processor. Color with 2 to 3 drops green food coloring.

Use as a sandwich spread or as a dip. Benedictine may also be used to stuff cherry tomatoes for an hors d'oeuvre tray.

Yields 2 cups.

Bistro Beef Sandwich

Red wine and roasted red peppers take this steak sandwich to new heights. Serves 4

1 pound beef round tip steak, 1/8 to 1/4-inch thick 2 cloves garlic, crushed

3 tablespoons lite soy sauce, divided 2 teaspoons olive oil

1 medium red onion, cut into thin wedges 1 1/2 cups sliced mushrooms

1 jar roasted red peppers, cut into strips 1/4 cup dry red wine

4 crusty rolls (6 inches each), split, toasted

Stack beef steaks, cut lengthwise in half and then crosswise into 1-inch strips. Heat large nonstick skillet over medium-high heat until hot.

Stir-fry beef strips and garlic (half at a time) 1-2 minutes or until outside surface is no longer pink. Remove from skillet and season with 2 tablespoons of the lite soy sauce and 1/8 teaspoon pepper.

In same skillet, heat oil over medium high until hot. Add onion and stir-fry 5 minutes. Add mushrooms and continue cooking 2-3 minutes or until vegetables are tender. Add red peppers, wine and remaining 1 tablespoon lite soy sauce. Bring to a boil and reduce heat. Return beef to skillet and heat through.

Serve beef mixture in rolls.

Black Forest Beef Sandwiches

3/4 cup applesauce

2 to 3 teaspoons prepared horseradish 2 tablespoons sliced green onions

pound flank steak

tablespoons butter or margarine 1/4 teaspoon salt

1/8 teaspoon pepper

4 slices lightly buttered rye bread toast 1 cup shredded lettuce

Sliced red onions Watercress

In bowl combine applesauce, horseradish and sliced green onions; set aside.

Slice steak diagonally across the grain, 1/8-inch thick.* In large skillet heat 1 tablespoon of the butter to sizzling. Add half the beef and sprinkle with half the salt and pepper. Toss over high heat until lightly browned. Remove and repeat with remaining butter, steak, salt and pepper.

For each serving: place a slice of toast on plate; cover with 1/4 cup of the lettuce and 1/4 of the beef slices. Serve the applesauce mixture on the side. Garnish with red onion rings and watercress.

* Partially freeze flank steak to make slicing easier. Makes 4 servings.

Beef Burgers

pound ground beef 3 teaspoons catsup

teaspoons mustard

1 small onion, chopped 1 teaspoon salt

1/2 cup bread, broken into small pieces 1/4 cup milk

1 1/2 teaspoons Worcestershire sauce

Mix all ingredients together. Broil in oven, or grill.

Bleu Cheeseburgers

1/4 pound bleu cheese

3 pounds lean ground beef 1/2 cup minced fresh chives

1/4 teaspoon hot pepper sauce

1 teaspoon Worcestershire sauce

1 teaspoon coarsely ground black pepper 1 1/2 teaspoons salt

1 teaspoon dry mustard 12 hamburger buns

Crumble the blue cheese into a large mixing bowl, and then thoroughly combine with ground beef, chives, hot pepper sauce, Worcestershire sauce, black pepper, salt, and mustard. Cover and refrigerate for 2 hours.

Preheat an outdoor grill for high heat. Lightly press the meat into about 12 patties. Cook on preheated grill until browned on both sides and to your desired doneness. Serve on hamburger buns.

Bourbon Franks

cup bourbon

1/4 cup brown sugar, packed

teaspoons Worcestershire sauce 1 cup catsup

1 tablespoon minced onion

1/8 teaspoon hot pepper sauce 2 to 3 pounds frankfurters

Combine all ingredients and simmer for 1 hour. Serve in hotdog buns.

Brats and Beer

4 bratwurst

1 cup beer 1/2 cup water

Dijon-style mustard Hot dog buns

Prepare grill to medium heat.

Pierce bratwurst three times with a fork. Place brats into a skillet. Add the beer and water. Cover and bring to a boil over high heat. Turn the temperature down and simmer Brats for 10 minutes. Remove from skillet.

Arrange the brats on an oiled, preheated grill. Grill for 5 to 6 minutes per side or browned. Take some left over beer and pour about 1/3 cup. Brush on Brats as they cook. Turn the brats only once. Brats are cooked when they are no longer pink in the center.

Remove from grill and place in hot dog buns. Add mustard and enjoy.

Brats 'n' Beer

1 (12 ounce) can or bottle beer (not dark) 4 bratwurst (about 1 pound)

1 sweet or Spanish onion, thinly sliced and separated into rings

1 tablespoon olive oil 1/4 teaspoon salt

1/4 teaspoon black pepper 4 hot dog buns

Prepare coals for direct grilling. Pour beer into heavy medium saucepan with ovenproof handle. (If not ovenproof, wrap heavy-duty foil around handle.) Place saucepan on grill. Pierce bratwurst with knife; add to beer. Simmer, uncovered, over medium coals, 15 minutes, turning once.

Place onion rings on heavy-duty foil. Drizzle with oil; sprinkle with salt and pepper. Fold sides of foil over rings to enclose. Place onion slices on grill. Grill, uncovered, 10 to 15 minutes or until onion slices are tender.

Transfer bratwurst to grill. Remove saucepan from grill; discard beer. Grill bratwurst, 10 minutes or until browned and cooked through, turning once. Place bratwurst in rolls. Top each with onions. Garnish as desired.

Brew Burgers

Brew Sauce

1/4 cup Heinz 57 Sauce 1/4 cup beer

In 1-cup glass measure, combine ingredients. Microwave on HIGH 1 to 1 1/2 minutes until bubbly; set aside.

Burgers

1 1/2 pounds ground beef

1 large sweet onion, 1/2-inch slices 4 slices Swiss cheese

4 crusty white or whole wheat rolls, split Lettuce

Shape ground beef into four 3/4-inch thick patties. Place onion slices on grid over medium, ash- covered coals. Grill onions, uncovered, 5 minutes.

Add patties; continue to grill, uncovered, 1 to 15 minutes or until onions are tender and burger centers are no longer pink, turning occasionally. Season burgers with salt after turning, if desired. Approximately 2 minutes before burgers are done, brush generously with sauce mixture; top with cheese.

Line bottom half of each roll with lettuce. Top each with burger, grilled onion and sauce. Close sandwiches

Cajun Chicken Sandwich

(6 ounce) boneless, skinless chicken breast halves, butterflied or pounded thin

tablespoons Cajun seasoning Butter

2 toasted buns, split

Preheat cast iron skillet over high heat on top of stove. Dredge chicken in Cajun seasoning. Place small amount of butter in skillet and place seasoned chicken breasts in skillet. Cook until seasoning is black, then turn and cook until done.

Serve on toasted bun with your favorite sandwich toppings. Makes 2 sandwiches.

Calico Sandwiches

6 English muffins

3 tablespoons margarine

(6 1/2 ounce) can tuna, drained 6 stuffed olives, chopped

hardboiled eggs, chopped 1/4 cup mayonnaise

1 celery stalk, chopped fine 1/8 cup pecan pieces

Slice English muffins lengthwise; toast, then butter. Mix all ingredients and put between the muffins.

California Chicken Cobb Sandwich

Two small loaves French bread

3 skinless, boneless chicken breast, grilled 12 pieces bacon, fried crisp

1 avocado, peeled and seeded 12 small, crisp lettuce leaves Dressing

4 ounces cream cheese, softened 6 tablespoons mayonnaise

4 ounces gorgonzola or blue cheese, softened Combine ingredients until mixed well.

To assemble sandwiches: Slice the bread into 24 thin slices; toast the bread lightly on both sides. Spread the inside of each piece of bread with sandwich dressing. Cut the grilled chicken breast into diagonal pieces to fit the small bread rounds. Top 12 pieces of bread and dressing with chicken, bacon pieces, avocado slices and lettuce. Top with remaining bread that has been spread with dressing.

Serve at once or cover with clean, dry lettuce leaves to keep moist.

California Club Sandwich

4 slices baked turkey breast 1 fresh tomato, sliced

4 slices crisp bacon

1/2 fresh avocado, sliced Alfalfa sprouts

slices whole wheat bread Miracle Whip

Toast bread; spread two bread slices with Miracle Whip. On one slice, arrange tomato slices and bacon. Add another slice of bread. Arrange avocado and alfalfa sprouts on bread. Add plain toasted slice of bread to top.

Camel Hump

pita breads Sliced cooked ham Sliced salami

2 tomatoes, sliced

2 tablespoons feta cheese, crumbled 1 tablespoon chopped ripe olives Lettuce

Dressing

1/4 cup Paul Masson® Rosé 2 tablespoons lemon juice 1/8 teaspoon oregano

1/8 teaspoon garlic salt 1/8 teaspoon turmeric 1/8 teaspoon pepper

Fill each pocket bread with sliced meats, tomatoes, cheese, olives and lettuce. Combine dressing ingredients and spoon over each sandwich before serving.

Makes 4 servings.

Candied Corned Beef Sandwiches

1 (4 pound) corned beef brisket

20 black peppercorns

bay leaves

tablespoons packed brown sugar 1 1/2 tablespoons soy sauce

1/2 teaspoon dry mustard 1 teaspoon ground ginger

tablespoons tomato ketchup 1 teaspoon red pepper flakes 1 teaspoon molasses

Place brisket in a pot and cover with water. Add peppercorns and bay leaves and bring to a simmer. Cook for 3 to 3 1/2 hours until fork tender, Set aside and make glaze.

Glaze

Drain corned beef and place on a foiled baking sheet. Preheat oven to 350 degrees F.

In a bowl, mix together sugar, soy sauce, mustard, ginger, ketchup, pepper flakes and molasses. Brush brisket with glaze. Bake for 15 to 20 minutes, re-glazing two times while baking.

Refrigerate overnight and slice across the grain very thin for sandwiches. Yield: 10 sandwiches

Carnitas

This is one thing you can do with extra pork roast. Serve with warmed flour tortillas, more lime juice and finely chopped avocado.

2 to 3 cups cooked pork roast pieces At least 1/2 cup chopped scallions Juice of 1 Mexican lime

1 to 2 tablespoons chopped garlic Salt and pepper, to taste

Preheat oven to 400 degrees F.

Combine all ingredients in a roasting pan coated with nonstick spray. Roast for 20 to 30 minutes on highest rack in oven. Then turn on broiler and broil about 5 minutes to desired shade of brown.

Makes 4 to 6 servings.

Carnival Corn Dogs

8 hot dogs

2 tablespoons cornmeal

1 tablespoon granulated sugar 1 cup pancake mix

2/3 cup water

Mix together cornmeal, sugar, pancake mix and water. Dip franks in batter, draining the excess over the bowl. Fry in deep fat for 2 to 3 minutes at 375 degrees F. Drain on paper towels.

Carolina Pulled Pork Sandwich

1/4 cup butter

1 1/2 cups chopped onion 3 cloves garlic, chopped

1 tablespoon powdered mustard 1 tablespoon paprika

teaspoon ground cinnamon 1 teaspoon cayenne pepper 2 cups catsup

1/4 cup packed dark brown sugar 1/4 cup apple cider vinegar

cups water

1 teaspoon salt

1/2 teaspoon ground black pepper 1 tablespoon vegetable oil

1 whole (5 pound) Boston pork butt 12 soft hamburger buns

Melt butter in saucepan. Add onion and garlic; cook until softened, 5 minutes. Add mustard, paprika, cumin and cayenne; cook 1 minute. Add catsup, sugar, vinegar and water; simmer, covered, 30 minutes. Uncover; simmer 30 minutes. Add salt and pepper. This can be made two days ahead, then refrigerated, covered. Before using, simmer 3 minutes.

Preheat oven to 350 degrees F. Heat oil in large ovenproof Dutch oven; add pork; brown for 10 minutes.

Bake, uncovered for 30 minutes. Pour 1 cup of barbecue sauce over pork. Cover pot. Lower heat to 250 degrees F. Bake 3 to 3 1/2 hours, basting meat occasionally, until a thermometer inserted in the middle of the roast registers 170 degrees F to 180 degrees F.

Let cool slightly. Trim off excess fat. Pull meat apart using two forks. Mix pulled meat with remaining barbecue sauce in a large bowl.

Serve on buns with cole slaw.

Cheese Flautas

In a pan a littler larger than a corn tortilla, melt enough shortening or lard to fill it 1/4 inch deep. With tongs dip a corn tortilla in the hot shortening or lard for a few seconds, just long enough so that it is soft and pliable. Remove and lay on a plate. Sprinkle grated Longhorn or Monterey Jack cheese down the center of the tortilla. Place 1 tablespoon tomato puree in the center of the cheese. Lay a strip of green chile about 1/2 inch wide on top of the cheese. Roll the tortilla up into a cigar-shape without pinching ends together. Fry until brown on both sides.

These are delicious served with guacamole and sour cream on the side

Cheese Sandwiches

1 jar Old English cheese spread 1/2 cup (1 stick) margarine

1 clove garlic, crushed

Mix well. Cut crusts from bread. Cut into halves or fourths. Cover top and sides with cheese spread. Bake 15 minutes at 350 degrees F.

These freeze well.

Cheesesteak Pockets

1 tablespoon vegetable oil 1 medium onion, sliced

1 (14 ounce) package frozen beef or chicken sandwich steaks, separated into 8 portions

1 can Campbell's Cheddar Cheese Soup

1 (4 1/2 ounce) jar sliced mushrooms, drained

4 (6-inch) pita breads, cut in half, forming two pockets

Heat oil in skillet. Add onion and cook until tender. Add sandwich steaks and cook until browned. Pour off fat. Ad soup and mushrooms and heat through. Spoon meat mixture into pita pockets.

Serves 4.

Cheesesteak Po'Boy

6 super-thin slices beef 2 teaspoons oil

Salt and pepper French loaf, split

3 slices mozzarella cheese

cup very thinly-sliced onions Preheat oven to 350 degrees F.

In a very hot skillet sear beef in 1 teaspoon of oil, about 30 seconds per side, or until just browned. Season with salt and black pepper. Stuff meat into open bread loaf. Top with cheese and bake until bread is slightly crispy and cheese is melted.

Meanwhile, heat remaining oil in the same skillet and sauté onions until tender. When sandwich is ready, top sandwich with onions.

Serve with potato chips. Yields 1 sandwich.

Cherry Chicken Salad Sandwich

cups cubed cooked chicken 1/2 cup dried tart cherries

green onions, sliced 1/2 cup mayonnaise 1/4 cup plain yogurt

1 tablespoon lemon juice

Freshly ground black pepper, to taste Lettuce leaves

Chopped fresh parsley 2 to 4 croissants

Combine chicken, cherries and onions in a large bowl; mix well. In another bowl, combine mayonnaise, yogurt, lemon juice and pepper; pour over chicken mixture. Mix gently. Refrigerate, covered, 1 to 2 hours.

Spoon chicken salad onto sliced croissants; top with lettuce. Garnish with parsley, if desired. Makes 2 to 4 servings, depending on size of croissants.

Chicken Cordon Bleu Calzones

4 boneless, skinless chicken breasts (1 pound) 1 cup sliced, fresh mushrooms

1/2 medium onion, chopped 3 tablespoons cornstarch

1 1/4 cups milk

1 tablespoon fresh basil or 1 teaspoon dried basil 1 teaspoon salt

1/4 teaspoon pepper

1 (17 1/2 ounce) package frozen puff pastry, thawed 8 thin slices deli ham

4 slices Provolone cheese

Place chicken in a greased 2-quart dish, cover with water. Cover and bake at 350 degrees F for 30 minutes or until juices run clear.

Meanwhile in skillet, saute mushrooms and onion in butter until tender.

Combine cornstarch and milk until smooth, stir into skillet mix. Add basil and seasonings. Bring to a boil, cook and stir for 2 minutes until thickened. Drain chicken.

Cut pastry sheets in half widthwise. On one side of each half, place a chicken breast, 1/4 cup mushroom mixture, two ham slices and one cheese slice. Fold pastry over fillings and seal edges. Place on a greased baking sheet. Brush tops with milk if desired. Bake at 400 degrees for 15-20 minutes or until puffed and golden.

Serves 4.

Chicken Crescents

3 ounces cream cheese 1 to 2 large cans chicken 1/2 teaspoon salt

1/8 teaspoon pepper 2 tablespoons milk

tablespoon chopped onion

tablespoons butter, softened 1/2 cup crushed croutons

2 tablespoons melted butter

Cream butter and cream cheese with milk, salt, and pepper. Blend in the chicken. Open crescent package, and create four rectangles with the crescents, don't tear them into triangles. Place 1/4 of chicken mixture in the center of each rectangle. Pull the corners up around the chicken and seal. Brush with butter, and top with crushed croutons. Bake 20 minutes at 350 degrees F.

Chicago Hot Dogs

All-beef hot dogs

Green sweet bell pepper, diced Yellow onions, diced

Mustard

Sweet pickle relish Dill pickle chips

Cucumbers, sliced thin Iceberg lettuce, shredded Tomatoes, diced

Hot peppers (pepperoncini) Celery salt

Steam hot dogs and put condiments on table. NEVER USE CATSUP! Celery salt is a MUST! Serve on poppy seed buns, if they are available.

Chicago-Style Italian Beef Sandwiches

(5 to 7 pound) rump roast 2 cups boiling water

beef flavor bouillon cubes 1 teaspoon dried marjoram 1 teaspoon thyme

1 teaspoon oregano

teaspoon hot pepper sauce, more or less, depending upon taste

Salt and pepper to taste

tablespoons Worcestershire sauce 6 garlic cloves, peeled and mashed 1/2 cup chopped green bell pepper

2 or more loaves Italian or Vienna bread, French

or any hard, crusty bread, sliced down the center, lengthwise, but not all the way through to the other side, then cut into serving size pieces

Place roast on a rack, in an open 13 x 9-inch roasting pan with the rack in it. Preheat oven to 325 degrees F. Bake, allowing 25 minutes per pound. Roast will be rare. Cool, and slice very thin.

To the drippings in the pan, add the boiling water, bouillon cubes or granules, (1 bouillon cube for each cup of boiling water used). Add marjoram, thyme, oregano, hot pepper sauce, salt, pepper, Worcestershire sauce, garlic cloves, and chopped green pepper. Simmer for 15 minutes.

Add the thinly sliced beef and cover. Marinate in gravy in refrigerator overnight.

The next day, heat thoroughly, and serve warm on the French bread, along with a crisp, green salad.

Makes 8 to 10 sandwiches.

Chicken a la King

1/4 cup melted butter 3 tablespoons flour

1 cup chicken broth 1 cup milk

teaspoon salt

cups diced cooked chicken 1 can mushrooms, drained 1/4 cup chopped pimento

Blend butter and flour in a frying pan. Blend in chicken broth and milk. Cook until thick. Add remaining ingredients and heat through. Serve over hot toast points.

If desired, you may add a few drops Tabasco to the sauce

Chicken Cordon Bleu Sandwiches

1 (10 ounce) package chicken patties

4 slices ham

4 slices Swiss cheese 4 buns

Mustard Lettuce Tomato

Prepare chicken according to package instructions. Top each chicken patty with a slice of ham and cheese. Return to oven for 2 minutes or until cheese is melted.

Spread buns with mustard. Assemble each sandwich with a patty, lettuce and tomato.

Chicken Pizza Burgers

Yield: 4 burgers

16 ounces ground chicken, fresh or thawed 2 cups pizza sauce, divided

1/2 teaspoon dried basil

4 slices provolone cheese 4 hot dog buns

Mix chicken, 2 teaspoons pizza sauce and basil in a bowl. Shape into 4 wide, hot dog- shaped patties. Grease grill, then heat. Cook for 9 to 10 minutes or until 165 degrees F in center. Top each with a cheese slice during the last few minutes of cooking.

Toast buns on cooler portions of grill. Heat remaining pizza sauce. Spread on toasted buns and top with patty

Chicken Salad Sandwich with Lemon-Herb Dressing

Makes 16 sandwiches.

1/4 cup mayonnaise 1/4 cup plain yogurt

tablespoon chopped fresh dill 1/2 teaspoon grated lemon zest
2 teaspoons lemon juice

1/4 teaspoon salt, or to taste

cooked whole boneless, skinless chicken breasts, cut into 1/4-
inch dice

4 lettuce leaves, optional 8 slices multigrain bread

Combine mayonnaise, yogurt, dill, lemon zest, lemon juice
and salt in a medium-size bowl. Add chicken pieces. Toss
with dressing. Place lettuce leaves on four slices of bread.
Divide chicken salad among four slices. Top with remaining
bread; cut each sandwich into four pieces.

Chicken Taco Pita Pockets

small avocado, thinly sliced 1 1/2 teaspoons lemon juice 1/4
teaspoon salt

cups finely cut-up cooked chicken

1 (4 ounce) can chopped green chiles, drained 1 small onion,
sliced and separated into rings 1 tablespoon vegetable oil

1/2 teaspoon salt

8 pita breads (about 3 1/2 inches in diameter)

2 cups shredded Monterey jack cheese (8 ounces) 1 cup shredded lettuce

1/2 cup sour cream 1/2 cup taco sauce

Sprinkle avocado slices with lemon juice and 1/4 teaspoon salt.

Mix chicken, chiles, onion, oil and 1/2 teaspoon salt in 1-quart microwavable casserole. Cover tightly and microwave on HIGH for 4 to 5 minutes, stirring after 2 minutes until chicken is hot.

Split each pita halfway around edge with knife. Separate to form pocket. Spoon about 1/4 cup of the chicken mixture into each pita. Top with cheese, lettuce and avocado.

Serve with sour cream and taco sauce. Makes 8 sandwiches.

Chile Rellenos Sandwiches

1 (4 ounce) can chopped green chiles, drained 6 slices bread

3 slices Monterey jack cheese 2 eggs

cup milk

to 4 tablespoons butter or margarine Salsa (optional)

Mash chiles with a fork; spread on three slices of bread. Top with cheese and remaining bread. In a shallow bowl, beat eggs and milk; dip the sandwiches.

Melt 2 tablespoons of butter in a large skillet. Cook sandwiches until golden brown on both sides and cheese is melted, adding additional butter if necessary.

Serve with salsa if desired. Yields 3 servings.

Chili Burritos

1 1/2 cups chili 4 flour tortillas

1 cup mild Cheddar cheese, grated

Heat the chili. Lightly heat the tortillas in a dry skillet. Divide the chili among the 4 tortillas. Sprinkle on the cheese. Roll up into cylinders. Serve warm.

Serves 4

Chili Dogs

1 (16 ounce) can chili or homemade chili 1 pound hot dogs

1/2 cup chopped onion

cup shredded Cheddar cheese

Heat chili in saucepan. Grill or broil hot dogs about 4 minutes. Put hot dogs on toasted hot dog rolls, top with chili, onion and cheese.

Chorizo/Beef Picadillo (Chorizo/Beef Filling)

1/2 tablespoons olive oil 2/3 cup green chiles, minced 2/3 cup onions, minced

2/3 cup potatoes, minced 3 cloves garlic, minced Heaping 1/4 teaspoon salt

Heaping 1/2 teaspoon ground cumin 1/2 teaspoon Mexican oregano

8 ounces chorizo

1 1/4 pounds very lean ground beef

Heat olive oil in a skillet over moderate heat and add green chiles, onions, potatoes and garlic. Sauté the vegetables until they are well browned, adjusting the heat as necessary, about 8 to 10 minutes, stirring often. You may have to add a little more olive oil to keep the vegetables from sticking.

Add tomatoes and continue cooking for 3 minutes, stirring often. Add salt, cumin and oregano and cook for 1 minute. Add chorizo, breaking it up and stirring it into the vegetables. When the chorizo has browned and released most of its fat, add the ground beef, breaking it up and mixing it with the other ingredients. When the ground beef has browned, cover the skillet, turn the heat to very low, and simmer, stirring occasionally, for 10 minutes.

Makes about 4 cups.

Coca-Cola® Sloppy Joes

1 1/2 pounds lean ground beef or turkey 1 large onion, chopped

1 cup Coca-Cola®

1 cup thick, tomato-based barbecue sauce 6 hamburger buns

In a nonstick skillet over medium-high heat, brown the beef or turkey with the onion until onion is soft and meat is no longer pink, about 5-10 minutes. Reduce heat to medium; stir in cola and barbecue sauce and continue to cook, stirring occasionally, until sauce is thickened to desired consistency, another 10-15 minutes. Season to taste with salt and pepper.

Toast cut side of buns, if desired, under broiler or in a skillet. Heap mixture onto buns. Serve. Makes 6 servings.

Per serving: 385 calories, (percent of calories from fat, 35), 27 grams protein, 34 grams carbohydrates, 2 grams fiber, 15 grams fat, 75 milligrams cholesterol, 645 milligrams sodium

Coconut Hot Dogs

Oil (for frying)

1/2 cup all-purpose flour 1/2 cup cornstarch

1 teaspoon salt

1/16 teaspoon white pepper 1 1/2 teaspoons oil

1/2 to 2/3 cup beer (at room temperature) 6 hot dogs

cup coconut, slightly chopped 3 tablespoons flour

Heat oil to 350 degrees F.

Combine flour, cornstarch, salt and pepper. Stir in 1 1/2 teaspoons oil and desired amount of beer so batter is not too thin. Coat hot dogs with batter, lifting out of batter with a fork. Sprinkle with coconut. Roll lightly in flour. Fry hot dogs one at a time in oil until golden. Heat in 275 degree F oven for 8 to 10 minutes until center of hot dogs are heated.

Colorful Pepper and Mango Quesadillas

teaspoons vegetable oil

1/2 red bell pepper, seeded and chopped 1/2 green bell pepper, seeded and chopped 1/2 yellow bell pepper, seeded and chopped 1/2 red onion, chopped

1 teaspoon chili powder

1 teaspoon oregano leaves

1 ripe but not too soft mango, peeled, seeded and chopped 1 tablespoon chopped cilantro

Juice of 1 lime

1 serrano or jalapeno chile, minced, or some crushed red pepper flakes to taste, optional

Flour tortillas (great to use two or three different colors/flavors)

Heat oil in large nonreactive skillet over medium heat. Add peppers, onions, chili powder and oregano. Sauté 2 minutes until softened. Add mango, cilantro, lime and hot pepper, if using. Stir to combine well; let cool.

Makes enough for about 3 (9-inch) quesadillas; each makes 3 to 4 appetizer servings or 2 entree servings.

For each quesadilla, spread 3/4 cup filling over the tortilla. Spread 2 tablespoons of your favorite salsa over the filling. Sprinkle 1/2 cup shredded cheese over the salsa and top with the second tortilla. Quesadillas can be assembled a day before cooking and stored stacked on a plate, covered well in your refrigerator. Bake quesadillas on a baking pan in a preheated 375 degree F oven 10 minutes or sauté them in a nonstick pan sprayed with no-stick cooking spray. Cook 2 minutes on each side until lightly browned and cheese is melted. After cooking, cut into 2-inch- wide wedges and garnish with cilantro sprigs.

Serve with salsa and sour cream.

12 kettle-cooked hot dogs

12 heated buns Mustard Chopped onion

Coney Sauce

1/2 pound ground beef 1/4 cup water

1/4 cup chopped onion 1/2 teaspoon MSG

1 garlic cloves, minced 8 ounces tomato sauce

1/2 teaspoon chili powder 1/2 teaspoon salt

Sauté the ground beef. Stir in remaining ingredients and simmer uncovered for 10 minutes.

Coney Island Hot Dogs

1 pound ground beef

4 tablespoons shortening 1 large onion, chopped

2 cups thick tomato purée 1 teaspoon cumin powder 1 teaspoon chili powder

1 clove garlic, minced 1 teaspoon salt

16 to 20 hot dogs

Brown beef in shortening, mashing as it cooks so meat will not be lumpy. Add onion when meat is half cooked. Add remaining ingredients, except hot dogs, and simmer about 30 minutes.

Serve hot with hot dogs and buns.

Corn Dogs

cup flour

tablespoons granulated sugar 1 1/2 teaspoons baking powder 1 teaspoon salt

2/3 cup cornmeal

2 tablespoons shortening 1 egg, lightly beaten

3/4 cup milk

1 pound hot dogs

Vegetable oil (for deep frying) Catsup

Prepared mustard

Sift together dry ingredients. Stir in cornmeal. Cut in shortening until mixture resembles coarse meal. Mix egg and milk and stir into cornmeal mixture until blended. Insert wooden Popsicle sticks into end of each hot dot. Coat evenly with batter. Fry in deep oil heated to 375 degrees F until brown.

Drain on paper towels and serve with catsup and mustard

Corned Beef Sandwich Spread

1 (12 ounce) can corned beef 1/2 cup celery

tablespoon grated onion Dash of salt

Dash of pepper

tablespoons relish

tablespoon horseradish

tablespoons mayonnaise

Corned Beef Sandwich Spread

4 tablespoons sharp cheese, grated 2 tablespoons mayonnaise

1/4 pound cooked corned beef, chopped 6 tablespoons minced sweet pickle

2 teaspoons finely minced onion 1 teaspoon prepared mustard 1/4 teaspoon salt

1/8 teaspoon pepper

Blend cheese and mayonnaise until smooth and soft. Add remaining ingredients. Mix until all ingredients are well blended. Store in refrigerator.

Makes 12 sandwiches.

Couzan Billy Burger

Well I did get to testing a new burger a while back...just haven't posted it yet. It is fairly unique and combines some tastes you may not think work. Give it a try......

Cut thick slices of red onion...about 1/2 inch for you onion lovers thinner for the rest of us!

Grill these over low heat and apply your favorite BBQ sauce to both sides. Be careful not to burn and over cook. Set these aside and cover loosely with foil.

Then prepare your burger as you normally would and toast your buns.

Place the onion slice on the bottom bun and then the burger and top with your favorite bleu cheese dressing. This topping can be homemade very easily. Here are a couple of ideas......

Mix bleu cheese with butter. Just enough butter to prevent the cheese from crumbling.

Mix bleu cheese with Mayo or sour cream, add some salt and pepper and a few drops of Tabasco sauce. I mix mine with Miracle Whip and Tabasco. again just enough to prevent the cheese from

crumbling. I do this in my little hand processor.

I will try to get more accurate measurements this weekend for the above bleu cheese dressings

Cowboy Joes

1 pound lean ground beef

1 (8 ounce) can tomato sauce 1/2 cup onion, chopped

1/4 cup catsup

1 tablespoon granulated sugar

1 1/2 teaspoons Worcestershire sauce 1 tablespoon vinegar

1/2 green bell pepper, chopped

In skillet, brown meat with pepper and onion; pour off fat. Add remaining ingredients except buns; bring to a boil. Reduce heat; cover and simmer 15 to 20 minutes.

Serve on buns.

Cowpoke Sandwich

1 large onion, sliced thick

Cilantro and Mexican oregano, dried, crumbled Salt and pepper

Bread slices, buttered

Vinegar and water, in equal amounts Cayenne pepper, to taste

Put onion slices in a bowl. Coat with spices, then cover with water and vinegar mixture. Refrigerate for 8 to 10 hours.

Drain onion slices, season with salt, pepper and cayenne. Place between two slices of buttered bre

Crab Benedict

pound fresh crabmeat, drained and flaked 1/2 cup chopped green bell pepper

1/2 cup chopped celery

tablespoons mayonnaise or salad dressing 1 tablespoon Worcestershire sauce

1 tablespoon butter or margarine, melted

1 (1 1/8 ounce) package Hollandaise sauce mix 4 English muffins, split and toasted

Combine first 5 ingredients; sauté mixture in melted butter until thoroughly heated. Prepare Hollandaise sauce according to package directions (or make your own!).

Spoon crabmeat mixture over cut sides of English muffins; top with Hollandaise sauce. Makes 4 servings.

Crab Burgers

cup fresh or canned crab meat 1/2 cup diced celery

tablespoons chopped onion

1/2 cup shredded Cheddar cheese 1/2 cup mayonnaise

Mix all ingredients. Spread on toasted English muffins and broil a few seconds. Serve hot.

Crab Melt Sandwiches

pound fresh lump crab meat, picked over 2 tablespoons fresh lime juice, or to taste 1/2 cup mayonnaise

teaspoons coarse-grained mustard

4 (1-inch thick) slices Italian bread, with crust removed 4 teaspoons freshly grated Parmesan

Unsalted butter, softened, if desired

Preheat broiler. Put crab meat in a bowl and add 1 tablespoon lime juice and toss to combine.

In a small bowl, whisk together remaining tablespoon lime juice, mayonnaise, and mustard until smooth. Pour sauce over crab and toss to coat. Season crab mixture with salt and pepper and chill, covered, for 30 minutes.

Lightly toast bread. Lightly butter toast. Spoon one fourth crab mixture into 1/2 cup measure. Holding toast on top of mixture in measure, invert crab onto the toast an set on an ungreased baking sheet. Repeat procedure with remaining crab mixture and toast and sprinkle 1 tablespoon Parmesan over each sandwich. Broil sandwiches about 3 inches from heat until cheese is melted and golden, 1 to 2 minutes.

Serves 4.

Crab Melt Sandwiches

pound fresh lump crab meat, picked over 2 tablespoons fresh lime juice, or to taste 1/2 cup mayonnaise

teaspoons coarse-grained mustard

4 (1-inch thick) slices Italian bread, with crust removed 4 teaspoons freshly grated Parmesan

Unsalted butter, softened, if desired Preheat broiler.

Put crab meat in a bowl and add 1 tablespoon lime juice and toss to combine. In a small bowl, whisk together remaining tablespoon lime juice, mayonnaise, and mustard until smooth. Pour sauce over crab and toss to coat.

Season crab mixture with salt and pepper and chill, covered, for 30 minutes.

Lightly toast bread. Lightly butter toast. Spoon one fourth crab mixture into 1/2 cup measure. Holding toast on top of mixture in measure, invert crab onto the toast an set on an ungreased baking sheet.

Repeat procedure with remaining crab mixture and toast and sprinkle 1 tablespoon Parmesan over each sandwich. Broil sandwiches about 3 inches from heat until cheese is melted and golden, 1 to 2 minutes.

Serves 4.

Crab Newburg

1 cup (2 sticks) butter

3 tablespoons flour

1/8 teaspoon red pepper Dash of Tabasco® sauce 2 tablespoons onion juice 2 cups heavy cream

1/2 teaspoon seasoned salt 1/2 teaspoon Accent®

In a double boiler, with water in bottom boiling vigorously, melt the butter. Blend in flour, stirring until mixture is smooth. Add remaining ingredients and cook until mixture is smooth, stirring constantly but slowly. The mixture should be thick.

Add 1 1/2 pounds crabmeat (if canned, wash in strainer to remove preservative, and pick out any cartilage). Heat thoroughly.

When sauce is thoroughly heated, add 3 tablespoons sherry wine, mix well, and let set while water in bottom pan simmers. Keep covered. Let steep for 15 minutes before serving over buttered toast or in patty shells.

Crab Tomato Sandwiches

3 ounces cream cheese, softened 1/2 cup shredded crabmeat

1 teaspoon lemon juice 1 egg, lightly beaten

3 tablespoons mayonnaise

2 tablespoons minced parsley

2 tablespoons grated Parmesan cheese Dash of cayenne pepper

6 slices sandwich bread, crusts removed 2 large tomatoes, ripe but firm

Preheat oven to boil. Combine cream cheese, crab meat, lemon juice, egg, parsley, Parmesan cheese and cayenne pepper; blend carefully. Toast one side of the bread slices. Cut tomatoes into thick slices and place on untoasted side of bread slices. Spread with the topping mixture and broil about 5 inches from heat until puffed and browned

Crabmeat Calzones

package hot roll mix 1 1/4 cups hot water

tablespoons vegetable oil 1 cup ricotta cheese

1 cup mozzarella cheese, grated 8 ounces cream cheese, softened 1/2 pound crabmeat

4 green onions, chopped 1 clove garlic, minced fine

1 small can olives, chopped

1 tablespoon fresh parsley or 1 teaspoon dried, chopped

In large bowl, combine hot roll mix (flour mixture and yeast). Moisten with water and oil. Turn out dough onto lightly floured surface. With greased hands, shape dough into ball and knead until no longer sticky (about 3 minutes). Divide into 10 equal parts. Cover loosely with plastic wrap and towel.

Meanwhile, combine remaining ingredients in medium bowl, mixing well.

Roll out each ball of dough into an 8-inch circle on a lightly floured surface. Spoon 1/3 cup filling over half of dough, coming within 1-inch of edge. Brush edge with water. Fold dough in half over filling. Press edges to seal, fluting sealed edge decoratively. Place on greased cookie sheet, then brush with oil. Bake at 400 degrees F until brown (about 25 to 30 minutes).

Variation: Make into an appetizer by folding filo dough wrapper around 1 tablespoon filling

Creamed Chicken on Toast

1 package grilled chicken breast strips (Louis Rich)

1 (10 3/4 ounce) can condensed cream of mushroom soup 1 1/2 cups broccoli florets, cooked drained

1/2 cup milk

1/2 cup shredded Swiss cheese 1 teaspoon Worcestershire sauce

8 slices bread, toasted cut diagonally in half

Sauté chicken breast strips in a nonstick saucepan with some vegetable spray, add soup, broccoli, milk, cheese and Worcestershire sauce cook on medium heat 5 minutes or until mixture is thoroughly heated and cheese is melted, stirring occasionally.

Serve over toasted bread slices.

Creamed Dried (Chipped) Beef Over Toast

2 tablespoons flour

cup milk

1/2 teaspoon Worcestershire sauce Dash of pepper

Blend until thick and creamy. Serve over buttered toast.

Creamed Shrimp on Toast

tablespoons flour

2 tablespoons butter

1 cup milk

Dash of white pepper Dash of salt

1 cup drained, canned shrimp or fresh, cooked shrimp

Blend flour and butter over low heat. Add milk, stirring constantly, until thickened. Add white pepper and salt. Then add shrimp and heat just until shrimp are heated.

Serve over toast.

Creamy Tuna on Bagels

8 ounces cream cheese, softened

1 (6 1/2 ounce) can tuna, drained, flaked 2 tablespoons scallion slices

1/2 teaspoon dill weed Dash of salt and pepper

3 bagels, sliced and toasted

Combine all ingredients except bagels; mix lightly. Spread bagel halves with cream cheese mixture. Broil for 5 to 7 minutes or until thoroughly heated.

Creole Bean Burger

1 (15 ounce) can red kidney beans, drained, rinsed and mashed

1 onion, chopped

1 egg

1 tablespoon catsup

teaspoon mustard

teaspoons Worcestershire sauce 1/4 teaspoon ground cumin

tablespoons flavored bread crumbs 1 tablespoon oil

hamburger buns Lettuce

Thousand Island dressing

Combine beans, onion, egg, catsup, mustard, Worcestershire sauce, cumin and bread crumbs. Form into 4 patties. Cook in oil in nonstick skillet for 3 minutes per side over medium-low heat.

Serve on buns with lettuce and Thousand Island dressing.

Creole Jack Rabbit

4 slices bacon, finely chopped 1/2 cup onion, minced

1/2 cup green bell pepper, minced 1/4 cup flour

cup milk

cups canned tomatoes, drained, chopped 1 cup Monterey jack cheese, shredded

1 teaspoon Worcestershire sauce 1/2 teaspoon salt

English muffins or toast triangles

Cook bacon until crisp. Add onion and green pepper and sauté until tender. Blend in flour. Stir in milk and tomatoes and cook until thickened. Add cheese, Worcestershire sauce and salt. Stir until cheese melts. Serve over toast or muffins.

Serves 6.

Crescent Cordon Bleu

1 1/2 cups chopped, cooked chicken 1 1/2 cups chopped, cooked ham

(6-ounce) jar sliced mushrooms or 1 cup fresh, sliced 4 ounces Swiss cheese, shredded

(8-ounce) cans crescent dinner rolls 1 egg, beaten

Sesame seeds

Preheat oven to 350 degrees F. Lightly coat a cookie sheet with vegetable cooking spray. In a bowl, combine chicken, ham, mushrooms and Swiss cheese.

Unroll dinner rolls, and separate each package into 4 rectangles, pressing perforations to seal. Spoon 1/2 cup mixture into center of each rectangle. Pull 4 corners of dough to center; twist slightly. Seal edges. Place on cookie sheet. Brush with beaten egg; sprinkle with sesame seeds.

Bake for 18 to 24 minutes until golden brown. Makes 8 servings.

Crescent Monte Cristo Loaf

2 (8 ounce) cans refrigerated crescent dinner rolls 2 tablespoons butter or margarine, melted

2 tablespoons honey

6 ounces thinly sliced smoked turkey

6 ounces thinly sliced Muenster cheese 6 ounces thinly sliced cooked ham

1/3 to 1/2 cup red raspberry preserves

Topping

2 tablespoons honey

1 tablespoon sesame seeds

Separate dough into 4 long rectangles. Place rectangles crosswise on 1 large or 2 small cookie sheets (rectangles should not touch), firmly press perforations to seal.

In small bowl, combine butter and 2 tablespoons honey, mix well. Brush over dough. Bake at 375 degrees F for 8 to 12 minutes or until golden brown; cool 15 minutes.

Grease a 15 x 10 x 1 inch baking pan. Carefully place one crust on pan. Top evenly with turkey. Place second crust over turkey; top with cheese and ham. Place third crust over ham; spread evenly with preserves. Top with fourth crust; brush top with 2 tablespoons honey and sprinkle with sesame seeds. Bake at 375 degrees F for 10 to 15 minutes or until loaf is deep golden brown. Let stand 5 minutes.

Cut into 6 to 8 slices.

Crock Pot Barbecue Beef

1 (2 1/2 pound) chuck roast

1 cup water

1 bottle barbecue sauce

1/3 cup Worcestershire sauce 1 teaspoon mustard

1 onion, chopped Salt and pepper

Add all ingredients to crockpot. Cook on HIGH heat until it boils. Simmer on LOW for 6 to 8 hours. Chop meat and stir all well. Serve.

Cuban Sandwich

Use leftover Roast Pork a la Criolla for this sandwich if you have any. This sandwich is a favorite in Miami, Florida, as it was first made by the Hispanic community there. Since it is eaten in the wee hours, after an evening of dancing and music, the Cuban Sandwich is sometimes known as "Medica Noche" (midnight), especially when made on the soft, sweet egg sandwich roll available from Cuban bakeries.

Split a Cuban or a submarine roll in half lengthwise; spread each roll half with prepared mustard and layer sandwich with one ounce each thinly sliced roast pork, Swiss cheese and deli ham; add sliced dill or bread and butter pickles and close sandwich. Lightly butter outside surface of roll and grill on a hot griddle or in a 400 degrees F oven until lightly toasted and cheese is melted

Cucumber Sandwiches

8 ounces cream cheese, softened

3 large cucumbers, shredded and drained

1 package Good Seasons Blue Cheese Dressing mix 1 tablespoon mayonnaise (not Miracle Whip)

Mix cheese, dry dressing mix and mayonnaise. Fold in cucumbers. Refrigerator sandwiches and leftover sandwich spread

Curried Shrimp Toast

12 slices firm white sandwich bread 1/2 cup soft butter

teaspoon curry powder

1/2 pound sharp Cheddar cheese, coarsely grated 12 to 16 ounces cooked shrimp

Remove crusts and toast bread on one side only.

Blend butter and curry and spread on untoasted side of bread.

Cut each into 4 squares and place on cookie sheet. Place one shrimp on each square. Lightly sprinkle and press in the cheese.

Toast carefully at 375 degrees F until cheese is melted (about 10 minutes). Serve hot

Davy Crocketts

Yields 4.

cans crescent rolls 1 pound ground beef

large onion, chopped

cans whole green chiles

to 2 cups shredded Mexican or Cheddar cheese 1/2 cup sour cream or to taste

or 3 stalks scallions, chopped Sliced black olives

Preheat oven to 375 degrees or the temperature required on the crescent roll can. Saute ground beef until no longer pink.

Open 1 can of crescent rolls and separate dough into rectangles and place them at least 1 inch apart on an ungreased cookie sheet.

Slit each of four green chiles down its length and open it up to flatten it. Lay one chile on each rectangle of crescent roll dough. Using a slotted spoon, spoon the drained ground beef equally over the 4 rectangles. Top each with chopped onion to taste. Top each with at least 1/4 cup cheese.

Open second can of rolls and separate into rectangles. Gently lay a rectangle over each Davy Crockett. You don't need to stretch the dough down to cover the edges. The dough will bake down and cover most of it. Bake as long as it says on the can to bake crescent rolls. Pass the sour cream, chopped green onion, shredded cheese and sliced olives so that each person may top their own Davy Crockett.

Denver Mile-High Taco Burger

1 pound lean ground beef

1 (1 ounce) envelope taco seasoning mix

Sliced Monterey jack cheese with hot peppers (pepper jack) 4 sandwich buns

Shredded lettuce Sliced tomato Mustard, to taste Catsup, to taste Mayonnaise, to taste Tortilla chips

Mix together ground beef and seasoning mix in a medium bowl. Form 4 patties. Grill to desired doneness. Place cheese on each burger and heat briefly to soften cheese. Serve burgers in buns with lettuce, tomato, condiments and chips

Deviled Hamburgers

1 pound ground chuck 1 teaspoon salt

1/4 teaspoon pepper 3 tablespoons catsup

1 teaspoon Worcestershire sauce 1 tablespoon minced onion

1 teaspoon mustard

1 teaspoon horseradish 1/4 cup dry bread crumbs 1 clove garlic, minced

Combine all ingredients and shape into 4 patties. Grill, fry, or broil as usual and enjoy.

Dilled Chicken Spread

1 cup chunk chicken, drained 1/4 cup mayonnaise

1 tablespoon chopped green onion 2 teaspoons prepared mustard

1/4 teaspoon dried dill Dash of pepper

Combine all ingredients. Makes about 1 cup.

Dill-icious Turkey Sandwich

1/2 tablespoons nonfat mayonnaise 2 teaspoons bottled capers, drained sprigs chopped fresh dill or 1/2 teaspoon dried dill 1/4 teaspoon freshly ground black pepper

2 pieces pumpernickel bread

2 slices fat free smoked turkey breast 3 thin slices cucumber

1 thin slice red onion

Combine mayonnaise, capers, dill and pepper, mixing well. Spread mixture evenly over bread. Layer with turkey, cucumber and red onion.

Makes 1 sandwich.

Dixie Bar-B-Que Sandwiches

medium onion, chopped

tablespoons butter or margarine 1 tablespoon vinegar

tablespoons brown sugar 1 cup ketchup

3 tablespoons Worcestershire sauce 1 tablespoon dry mustard

1 cup water

1/2 cup celery, chopped Salt and pepper to taste

1 to 1 1/2 pounds cooked, shredded pork 4-6 sandwich buns

Combine all ingredients except pork in a saucepan. Cook slowly until flavors are blended and butter is melted, about 15 minutes. Stir in pork. Serve on buns.

Makes 4-6.

Dogs in Blankets

8 skinless hot dogs Flour

1/4 cup cornmeal 1/4 teaspoon salt

1/4 teaspoon baking soda 1 egg

1/2 cup buttermilk

Fat for frying (part bacon, part lard)

Put wooden skewer in each hot dog. Roll in flour and shake off excess. Sift 1/2 cup flour and next 3 ingredients into bowl. Add egg and buttermilk and beat with whisk to form a smooth thick batter. Holding skewer, dip hot dog in batter, coating well. Drop into hot deep fat (375 degrees F to 400 degrees F) and fry until golden brown.

Drain on paper towels and serve at once with mustard.

Easy BBQ Beef Sandwiches

1 (3- to 5-pound) chuck roast 1 can ginger ale

1 1/2 cups ketchup

Using an electric skillet brown beef on both sides. Mix ketchup and ginger ale together and pour over the browned beef. Cook for 7 hours at 200 degrees F. All the fat will separate and the ginger ale and ketchup will make a thick barbecue sauce.

Easy Crescent Dogs

8 Oscar Mayer Beef Franks or Wieners 4 Kraft Singles Process Cheese Food,

each cut into 4 strips

1 (8 ounce) can Pillsbury Crescent Rolls

Cut a lengthwise pocket into each beef frank to within 1/2-inch of ends; insert 2 cheese food strips into each pocket.

Separate crescent roll dough into triangles; wrap 1 triangle around each frank. Place on ungreased cookie sheet, cheese side up. Bake in preheated 375 degree F oven for 12 minutes or until golden brown

Egg Salad

6 hardboiled eggs, grated fine or sieved 1/3 cup minced pimento-stuffed olives 1/4 cup plus 1 tablespoon mayonnaise 2 tablespoons minced scallions

2 tablespoons minced parsley

1 tablespoon prepared Dijon mustard Salt and freshly-ground black pepper Lettuce leaves

Combine all ingredients in a medium bowl, and mix thoroughly. Refrigerate, covered, at least 30 minutes.

Leftovers can be kept a couple of days. Makes about 2 cups.

Egg Salad

This is the best recipe I have found for Egg Salad. The flavor is wonderful.

8 (10-minute) hard boiled eggs (11 minutes out of refrigerator)
1/2 cup red sweet onions, diced)

3 garlic cloves, minced finely

1 1/2 teaspoons kosher course salt

1 teaspoon fresh ground black pepper 1 cup mayonnaise

1/4 cup fresh basil (cut into strips)

After boiling eggs, chill in ice water for 15 minutes. Peel off the shells. Blend all ingredients together.

Serve on bread or toast.

Elvis Presley's Fried Peanut Butter and Banana Sandwich

1 small ripe banana 2 slices white bread

3 tablespoons peanut butter 2 tablespoons butter

In a small bowl, mash the banana with the back of a spoon. Toast the bread lightly. Spread the peanut butter on one piece of toast and the mashed banana on the other. Fry the sandwich in melted butter until each side is golden brown.

Cut diagonally and serve hot.

Fiesta Steak Sandwich

1 strip steak

1 hoagie roll Sliced avocado Sliced tomato Shredded lettuce

Prepare strip steak by pan frying or broiling. Prepare Fiesta Mayo while steaks are cooking. Place a sliced Cheddar or jack cheese on the steak during the last minute of cooking to melt.

Fiesta Mayo

1/2 cup mayonnaise

1/2 teaspoon garlic powder

1/2 teaspoon crushed red pepper

1 teaspoon fresh finely diced cilantro 1 teaspoon lime juice

Mix all ingredients together until creamy.

Toast a hoagie roll. Spread fiesta Mayo on both sides of the bun. Place the steak with cheese on the bottom side of the roll. Top with sliced avocado, tomato and lettuce, then add the top side of the roll.

Fluffernutter

This is a very old recipe.

Marshmallow Fluff

Peanut butter (smooth or creamy) 2 slices bread

Spread peanut butter onto one slice of bread. Cover with Marshmallow Fluff. Top with second slice of bread and enjoy!

Frank Blandi's Original Devonshire Sandwich

Cream Sauce

3/4 stick butter, melted 1 cup all-purpose flour

1/4 pound Cheddar cheese, grated 1 pint chicken broth

1 pint hot milk 1 teaspoon salt

Melt butter in deep pan and add flour, stirring constantly. Add chicken broth and then hot milk, stirring all the while. Add cheese and salt. Bring to boil, then cook slowly for 20 minutes, still stirring. Cool to lukewarm. Beat with wire whip until smooth before using. This makes enough sauce for 6 Devonshire sandwiches.

For each sandwich

1 slice toast, crusts trimmed off 3 slices crisp bacon

5 thin slices cooked turkey breast Cream Sauce, recipe above Melted butter

Parmesan cheese and paprika Preheat oven to 450 degrees F.

In each flat, individual ovenproof casserole dish, place 1 slice of toast and top with 3 slices bacon. Add 5 thin slices of cooked turkey breast. Cover completely with cream sauce. Sprinkle with a little melted butter, then with the combined Parmesan cheese and paprika. Bake 10 to 15 minutes or until golden brown.

French Dip Sandwich

1 can Franco-American Au Jus Gravy

4 servings thinly sliced cooked roast beef 4 servings French bread or long

hard rolls, cut in half lengthwise

In 10-inch skillet, combine gravy and beef. Over low heat, heat through, stirring occasionally.

To make sandwiches, arrange beef on bread. Serve each sandwich with small bowl of gravy for dipping.

French Dip Sandwich with au Jus

1 (3 pound) beef chuck roast, trimmed 2 cups water

1/2 cup soy sauce

1 teaspoon dried rosemary 1 teaspoon dried thyme

1 teaspoon garlic powder 1 bay leaf

3 peppercorns (3 to 4) 8 French rolls, split

Place roast in a slow cooker. Add water, soy sauce, and seasonings. Cover and cook on HIGH for 5-6 hours or until beef is tender.

Remove meat from broth; shred with forks and keep warm. Strain broth; skim off fat. Pour broth into small cups for dipping. Serve beef on buttered and toasted rolls.

Servings: 8

French Dip Sandwiches

1 long loaf French bread

1/2 pound cooked roast beef (from deli or leftovers) 1 package roast beef au jus gravy

4 tablespoons butter

teaspoon garlic powder

Cut French bread in half lengthwise. Spread with butter and sprinkle with garlic. Wrap in foil and heat in oven until warm. Mix gravy as directed on package and warm beef in juice. Drain beef from gravy and put on bottom of warm bread. Put top on sandwich and slice. Put gravy into small bowls (one for each person). Dip sandwich in gravy to eat.

Serve with French fries and a salad.

French Onion Sandwiches

Yield: 4 servings

tablespoons butter or margarine 4 (4 ounce) beef cube steaks

1 medium onion, sliced and separated into rings 1 cup beef broth

tablespoon cornstarch

teaspoons Worcestershire sauce 1/8 teaspoon garlic powder

Dash of pepper

4 (1-inch) slices French bread, toasted 2 (1-ounce) slices Swiss cheese, halved

In a large skillet melt butter. Add steaks and cook over medium-high heat for 2 to 3 minutes on each side or until done. Remove from skillet, reserving drippings.

Cook onion in drippings until tender.

Combine broth, cornstarch, Worcestershire sauce, garlic powder and pepper. Add to skillet. Cook and stir until bubbly. Cook and stir 2 minutes more.

Place steaks on bread. Top with cheese and onion mixture.

Fried Catfish Sandwiches with Bacon, Lettuce and Tomato

Sauce

3/4 cup mayonnaise

3 tablespoons sweet pickle relish

1 1/2 tablespoons drained bottled capers, chopped fine 1 tablespoon Dijon-style mustard

1 tablespoon fresh lemon juice, or to taste A pinch of cayenne

tablespoon bottled cocktail sauce, or to taste

All-purpose flour seasoned with salt and pepper for dredging the fish

large eggs

1/2 teaspoon salt

1/4 teaspoon cayenne Cornmeal for dredging the fish

4 (1/2 pound) catfish fillets, halved crosswise Vegetable oil for deep-frying the fish

8 soft sandwich rolls, split

Soft-leafed lettuce for the sandwiches 2 tomatoes, sliced thin

16 slices lean bacon, cooked

Make the sauce: In a bowl stir together the mayonnaise, the relish, the capers, the mustard, the lemon juice, the cayenne, the cocktail sauce, and salt and pepper to taste and chill the sauce, covered.

Have ready in separate shallow dishes the flour, the eggs beaten with the salt and the cayenne, and the cornmeal. Dredge each catfish fillet half in the flour, shaking off the excess, dip it in the egg mixture, letting the excess drip off, and dredge it in the cornmeal. Transfer the fish as it is coated to a wax paper-lined baking sheet.

In a kettle heat 1 inch of the oil to 375 degrees F on a deep-fat thermometer. In it fry the fish in batches for 2 to 4 minutes on each side, or until it is cooked through and the coating is crisp, and transfer it with a slotted spatula to paper towels to drain.

On the bottom halves of the rolls layer the lettuce, the tomatoes, the bacon, the fish, the sauce, and the top halves of the rolls.

Serves 8.

Fried Green Tomato Sandwiches

1 (8 ounce) package sliced bacon 1 large egg white

1/4 teaspoon salt 1/2 cup cornmeal

1/2 teaspoon coarsely ground black pepper

pound green tomatoes (3 medium), cut in 1/2-inch slices 1/4 cup low-fat mayonnaise dressing

1/4 cup low-fat plain yogurt

tablespoons chopped fresh chives 4 green-leaf lettuce leaves

8 slices firm whole-grain or white bread, toasted Cook bacon. Drain on paper towels.

Meanwhile, in pie pan, beat egg white and salt. In another pie pan, combine cornmeal and 1/4 teaspoon pepper. Dip tomato slices in egg-whites to coat both sides, then dip in cornmeal to coat both sides well. Place on waxed paper.

In bacon drippings in skillet, cook tomato, a few at a time, over medium-high heat until golden brown and heated through, about 3 minutes. Drain.

In small bowl, combine mayonnaise, yogurt, chives, and 1/4 teaspoon pepper. Spread on toast. Arrange lettuce, tomatoes, and bacon between toast slices.

Fried Peanut Butter and Jelly Sandwiches

2 eggs, slightly beaten 1/2 teaspoon salt

1/2 cup milk 12 slices bread

1/2 cup smooth peanut butter 1/4 cup shortening

Jelly

Combine eggs, salt and milk. Spread 6 slices of bread with peanut butter. Top with remaining slices of bread and cut in half diagonally. Dip sandwiches in egg mixture and fry on preheated, well-greased griddle until golden brown on both sides.

Serve hot with jelly.

Garden Fresh Calzones

Vegetable oil cooking spray 3/4 cup mushrooms, sliced

3/4 cup zucchini, halved lengthwise, thinly sliced 1/4 cup red bell pepper, diced

1/4 cup yellow bell pepper, diced 1/4 cup green onion, sliced

1/4 teaspoon garlic powder 1/2 teaspoon Italian seasoning

1 (10 ounce) can refrigerated pizza crust dough 4 tablespoons light mozzarella cheese

4 tablespoons light spaghetti sauce 1 egg white, beaten

Preheat oven to 425 degrees F. Spray cookie sheet with cooking spray.

In a medium mixing bowl combine mushrooms, zucchini, peppers and onion. Sprinkle with garlic powder and Italian seasoning; mix well. Unroll pizza dough onto cookie sheet. Roll dough into large square. Cut into 4 equal squares. Place 1 tablespoon cheese, 1 tablespoon sauce and 1/4 vegetable mixture on each square, leaving a 1/2-inch edge on each square. Fold dough in half over filling. Press edges with fork to seal. Brush with egg white and make 3 slits on top of each calzone. Bake 12 to 15 minutes or until golden brown.

Garlic Bread with Philly Steak

1 loaf French bread

1 1/2 pounds thin strips round steak 1 large bell pepper

1 1/2 pounds mushrooms 1 large red onion

4 cloves garlic, minced 1 teaspoon sage

Salt and pepper to taste

Garlic Bread

1/2 pound butter 1/8 cup olive oil Garlic powder Paprika

Pepper

Grated cheese to taste Sprinkle of Italian seasoning

Cut meat into 3 x 1/2-inch strips. Cut the bell pepper the same way. Cut mushrooms into slices. Slice onion thinly and mince garlic finely.

Pan brown the meat at medium high for about 10 minutes. Add remaining ingredients. Lower heat and sauté for about 10 to 15 minutes until a nice, beefy sauce is made in the pan.

Serve on garlic French bread.

Garlic Bread: Slice bread in half lengthwise. Butter both cut sides. Add remaining ingredients, sprinkling evenly on both halves. Microwave 30 seconds or heat in the oven 5 minutes.

Serve with "Philly" steak or a side dish.

Giant Meatball Sandwich

pound ground beef

1/2 pound ground pork sausage

cups commercial spaghetti sauce with peppers and mushrooms

1 clove garlic, minced

1 (16 ounce) loaf unsliced Italian bread

1 (6 ounce) package sliced provolone cheese

Combine ground beef and sausage; shape into 1-inch balls. Cook in a large skillet over medium- high heat for 8 to 10 minutes or until browned. Remove from heat; drain meatballs on paper towels. Discard drippings.

Combine spaghetti sauce and garlic in skillet; add meatballs. Cook over medium heat, stirring occasionally, 12 to 15 minutes or until done. Cut bread in half lengthwise. Place on a baking sheet, cut sides up; broil 5 inches from heat for 2 minutes or until lightly toasted.

Spoon meatball mixture onto bottom half of bread. Cut cheese slices in half; arrange on top of meatballs, overlapping as needed. Place top half of bread over cheese.

Serve immediately.

Glop

This is an old old old family recipe. Even today, at the right time, I love it.   My mother called it

GLOP. We never bothered to change the name; it wasn't necessary.

pound Tillamook cheese 1 small can tomato sauce A pinch of garlic salt

Dash of oregano Dash of marjoram

Sliced pepperoni, cut into thin strips and/or cut-up mushrooms (optional)

Grate cheese into a bowl. Add all other ingredients and stir thoroughly.

Spread mixture on open hamburger buns and broil until toasty and cheese is melted and optional ingredients are heated through.

Grands Tuna Melts

(6 ounce) cans water-packed tuna, well drained 1/3 cup chopped onion

1/3 cup mayonnaise 1/8 teaspoon salt 1/8 teaspoon pepper

1 (1 pound 1.3 ounce) can Pillsbury Grands Refrigerated Flaky Biscuits 4 ounces (1 cup) shredded Cheddar cheese

Sour cream, if desired Chopped tomato, if desired Shredded lettuce, if desired

Preheat oven to 350 degrees F. Grease cookie sheet.

In medium bowl, combine tuna, onion, mayonnaise, salt and pepper; mix well.

Separate dough into 8 biscuits. Place 4 biscuits on greased cookie sheet. Press or roll each to form a 5-inch round. Spoon tuna mixture into center of biscuits. Top each with cheese. Press or roll remaining 4 biscuits to form 5-inch rounds. Place over filling. Press edges to seal.

Bake for 15 to 20 minutes or until golden brown.

Cut each sandwich in half. Top each with sour cream, tomato and lettuce.

Greek Quesadilla

flour tortilla

tablespoons feta cheese

1/4 cup shredded mozzarella cheese

Pinch of finely diced herbs (oregano, basil and rosemary) 3 tablespoons diced Kalamata olives

1/8 cup finely diced onion

Sprinkle ingredients evenly over one side of the tortilla. Fold in half. Grill for about 1-2 minutes, or bake at 350 degrees F for 5 minutes. Slice in thirds and serve.

Greek Salad Heroes

3/4 cup thinly sliced fresh mushrooms 1/2 cup thinly sliced cucumber

2 tablespoons ripe olives

2 tablespoons crumbled feta cheese 1 tablespoon white balsamic vinegar 1/8 teaspoon dried oregano

2 Roma or small tomatoes, thinly sliced 1 clove garlic, minced

2 (2 1/2 ounce) submarine rolls

2 lettuce leaves

6 slices baked cooked ham

6 slices honey roasted smoked turkey

Combine first 8 ingredients in a small bowl; toss gently. Let stand for 30 minutes, tossing occasionally.

Cut a thin slice off top of each roll and set aside.

Cut a 2-inch wide, V-shape wedge down the length of each roll (as they do at Subway). Reserve bread wedges for another use.

Drain vegetable mixture. Line each roll with a lettuce leaf; arrange ham and turkey evenly over lettuce.

Spoon vegetable mixture evenly over meat and cover with roll tops.

Green Chili Burger

A burger that will make you say olé! Prep: 10 minutes Cook: 5 minutes

Servings: Serves 4

4 fully cooked burger patties 1/2 small sweet onion

1 tablespoon butter

1 (4 ounce) can whole green chilies, drained 4 slices Monterey jack or pepper jack cheese 4 Kaiser rolls or hamburger buns

Salsa picante

Heat burgers in microwave according to package directions. Cut onion into 1/4-inch thick slices.

Heat butter in a large skillet over medium heat. Grill onions about 2 minutes on each side, until soft and golden.

Meanwhile, split green chilies and lay flat over top of burger. Lay 1 slice cheese over each; return to microwave briefly to melt cheese.

Heat buns in microwave or oven until warm. Spread salsa on buns. Place burger patties on buns and top with grilled onions

Grilled Cheese with Ham and Tomato

When I want to be more elaborate with grilled cheese and really make a meal of it I use this recipe.

Potato bread slices Deli boiled ham Muenster cheese Cheddar cheese Sliced tomatoes

To each sandwich I add ham, muenster and cheddar cheese and a sliced tomato. I fry in butter. Serve with salads and pickles and pork 'n' beans. In the winter I also serve with soup.

Grilled Chicken Sandwich with Roasted Red Onion and Garlic Mayonnaise

Serving size: 6

Garlic Mayonnaise

3 slices red onion (1/2-inch slices), roasted 1 head garlic, roasted

2 tablespoons olive oil

Sandwich

loaf focaccia bread, sliced 1/2 cup olive oil, for marinade

boneless chicken breast halves, grilled and sliced 5 portobello mushrooms, grilled and sliced

1 1/2 tablespoons olive oil, for sautéing 2 tablespoons garlic, finely minced

6 cups fresh spinach, cleaned

1/4 pound gruyere cheese, thinly-sliced

Garlic Mayonnaise: Cut top off garlic to expose cloves. Slice onion. Drizzle with olive oil. Roast at 375 degrees F for 40 minutes. Add to basic mayonnaise and blend until smooth.

Sandwich: Marinate the chicken and mushrooms in olive oil for 10 minutes. Grill over high heat, and then slice.

In hot sauté pan, cook garlic in oil for 15 seconds. Add all the cleaned spinach. Compact the spinach, toss and stir. Cook just till wilted.

lice Focaccia to form a top and a bottom. Lightly brush each cut side with olive oil. Place both pieces under your broiler so that the cut side is toasted.

Layer ingredients like spokes on a wheel. This spreads them out evenly so there's filling in every bite. Start with chicken, then spinach, then mushrooms, and finally cheese.

After adding the cheese, run the sandwich under broiler to melt cheese. Add plenty of the mayonnaise and replace top.

Serve by cutting into 6 pie-shape wedges.

Grilled Eggplant Burgers

6 slices peeled eggplant, 1/2 inch thick 2 tablespoons olive oil

4 ounces goat cheese

1/4 cup sun dried tomatoes in oil 1/4 cup pine nuts

12 thin slices good quality bread, toasted

Grill, broil or sauté the slices of eggplant that have been brushed with oil until brown and soft. Place the eggplant slices on the bread and top with goat cheese, sun dried tomatoes and pine nuts. Top with remaining slices of bread and serve.

Grilled Garlic Steak Sandwiches

1 1/2 cups butter or margarine

30 cloves garlic, minced (about 2/3 cup) 5 large red bell peppers

5 large green bell peppers

3 large (about 1 1/2 pounds total) onions 3 flank steaks, each 1 1/4 to 1 1/2 pounds

Blend butter and 1/3 of the minced garlic. Clean and cut peppers in strips. Coarsely chop onions.

Divide peppers, onions, and remaining garlic evenly between two 5 to 6-quart pans. To each pan add 3 tablespoons garlic butter mixture. Place pans over medium-high heat. Stir often until vegetables are browned and onions taste sweet, about 30 minutes; keep warm.

Place flank steaks on grill, turning frequently until desired doneness, allowing 10 to 14 minutes for rare.

Transfer steaks to cutting board and tent with foil to keep warm. Toast rolls on grill.

Cut the steaks thinly across the grain. Fill rolls equally with sliced steak and pepper-garlic mixture.

Serve with a variety of salads and grilled corn on the cob. Corn on the cob can be served hot or tepid, with a variety of toppings such as honey butter, pesto, lime wedges and salt and spreadable herbed cheese (such as Rondele or Boursin).

Grilled Ham and Brie Sandwiches

12 slices pumpernickel bread Creole mustard

1 pound thinly sliced smoked ham (Virginia ham from the deli is good) 1 pound thinly sliced Brie cheese

1/2 cup butter, room temperature (or use the stuff in the plastic tub)

Butter one side of each slice of bread. Turn six of them butter down side on the counter. Spread with mustard then layer with ham and Brie. Spread other six slices with mustard, on unbuttered side ya know. Put mustard side down on other stuff. Heat pan or griddle to medium heat and grill sandwiches. When brown to your likin', turn them over and grill again. Eat.

Grilled Hamburgers

8 hamburger patties

1 tablespoon dry mustard

1 tablespoon Worcestershire sauce 1/2 cup melted butter or margarine Juice of 2 lemons

Combine mustard, Worcestershire, butter and lemon juice. Marinate patties for several hours before grilling

Grilled Peanut Butter and Bananas

Peanut butter

4 English muffins, sliced in half 2 medium bananas

Butter or margarine, softened

Spread peanut butter over one side of 4 slices bread; slice bananas and arrange on top. Top with remaining bread. Spread top slices with butter or margarine. Place sandwiches, margarine sides down, in skillet. Spread top slices with margarine.

Cook uncovered over medium heat until bottoms are golden brown, about 4 minutes; turn. Cook until bottoms are golden brown and peanut butter is melted, 2 to 3 minutes longer.

Grilled Quesadillas

4 tortillas

1 cup Monterey jack cheese, shredded

1 cup stemmed, coarsely chopped watercress or arugula 1 tablespoon thinly sliced red onion

1 tablespoon tomato, finely chopped 1 tablespoon garlic (optional)

1 serrano or jalapeño pepper, finely chopped Salt and pepper to taste

Lightly oil the grill rack and place it about 4 inches above the coals.

Over medium heat, grill the tortillas for about 1 minute. Turn over and sprinkle with the remaining ingredients. Cover loosely with heavy-duty foil (or the grill hood) and cook until cheese melts (about 1 minute), checking to ensure that tortillas do not burn.

To serve, remove from grill and cut into wedges. Serve with salsa, guacamole or sour cream.

Grilled Rachel

12 large slices dark rye bread Mayonnaise or salad dressing

2 pounds cooked turkey breast, thinly sliced 1 (16 ounce) can sauerkraut, well drained 12 slices Swiss cheese

Butter or margarine, softened

For each sandwich, use 2 slices bread, one-sixth of the turkey slices, one-third cup sauerkraut and 2 slices cheese.

Assemble sandwiches by spreading one side of each bread slice with mayonnaise. On six bread slices, layer turkey, sauerkraut and cheese. Cover with remaining bread slices, mayonnaise side down. Spread top bread slice evenly with softened butter; place buttered side down in skillet.

Butter other bread slice. Cover; grill slowly on each side. Makes 6 sandwiches.

Grilled Reuben Chicken Melts

Yields 4.

4 skinless boneless chicken breast halves 2 cups shredded red cabbage

1 1/2 cups (6 ounces) Swiss cheese, shredded 1 large onion, cut into 1/2-inch slices

1 1/4 cups Thousand Island salad dressing, divided 4 French rolls, split

Brush chicken and onion with 1/2 cup salad dressing; set aside. Combine 1/4 cup salad dressing and cabbage; mix well; set aside.

Grill chicken over hot coals 5 to 7 minutes on each side or until no longer pink in center. Sprinkle chicken evenly with Swiss cheese during the last minute of grilling.

Grill onion 4 to 5 minutes on each side, or until browned and tender.

Grill rolls until toasted. Spread toasted sides of rolls with remaining 1/2 cup salad dressing. Place chicken on roll bottoms. Top with onion, cabbage mixture and roll tops. Serve immediately.

Grilled Salmon Burgers

(15 1/2) ounce) can salmon 1/4 cup uncooked oatmeal 1/2 cup corn flake crumbs

tablespoons mayonnaise 1/3 cup chopped onions

2 tablespoons lemon juice 1 egg

2 teaspoons horseradish

Mix well. Make into four large or six small patties. Grill over a finely meshed grill screen on the barbecue grill or broil fairly far away from the heat in a broiler for about six minutes on each side.

Serve on buns. These are delicious!

Grilled Vegetable Heros

2 large zucchini, sliced lengthwise

2 tablespoons chopped fresh basil, plus

large red bell pepper, quartered lengthwise and seeded 8 large basil leaves

Italian sandwich rolls with, split lengthwise (horizontally) 1 large firm tomato, cut into 4 slices

Salt, to taste

Freshly-ground black pepper, to taste

6 tablespoons bottled Italian salad dressing 4 thin slices Provolone cheese

Prepare grill (medium-high heat). Arrange zucchini, bell pepper and tomato on rimmed baking sheet. Whisk dressing and chopped basil in medium bowl to blend. Brush cut side of each roll with 1/2 tablespoon dressing mixture. Brush vegetables with remaining dressing mixture and sprinkle with salt and pepper.

Grill cut side of rolls until toasted, about 1 minute. Place rolls, cut-side up, on plates. Grill vegetables until tender and lightly charred, turning and brushing occasionally with any dressing mixture left on baking sheet, about 10 minutes.

Arrange warm vegetables on roll bottoms. Cover each with 2 slices cheese, 4 whole basil leaves and top of roll.

Yields: 2 servings

Grinder

French loaf, split 3 slices salami

3 slices mortadella

3 slices provolone cheese 3 slices Swiss cheese

10 rings pickled banana peppers or pepperoncini Olive oil

Preheat oven to 350 degrees F.

Open up loaf and layer all ingredients inside. Drizzle with olive oil, then bake until warm and crispy.

Guacamole BLT

Serves 12.

1 1/2 pounds bacon

4 ripe avocados (1 1/2 pounds), pitted and peeled Juice of 1/2 lime

Focaccia

Oven-dried tomatoes

1 to 2 heads Bibb lettuce, leaves separated, or 1/2 head Boston lettuce

3/4 cup homemade mayonnaise, or prepared

Cook bacon until browned and crisp. Transfer bacon to a paper-towel-lined pan to drain; discard fat.

Place avocadoes in a bowl with lime juice, and mash with a fork until chunky but spreadable.

Using a large serrated knife, split focaccia horizontally. Spread bottom with avocado mixture; layer with bacon, oven-dried tomatoes, and lettuce. Spread remaining focaccia with mayonnaise, and top sandwich.

Cut into 12 squares and serve.

NOTE: This is wonderful made with roasted garlic mayonnaise.

Guacamole Burger

Serves 12.

1 tablespoon Worcestershire sauce 1 tablespoon salt

1/2 tablespoon pepper

1 1/2 pounds lean ground beef 4 onions, sliced

4 tomatoes

3 California avocados, seeded, peeled and mashed Lettuce leaves as needed

12 sesame burger buns

Combine Worcestershire, salt, pepper, and ground beef. Shape into 12 patties. Refrigerate at least 30 minutes.

Broil, grill, or pan fry to desired doneness. Serve on bun with lettuce, sliced tomatoes, and onion. Place approximately 2 ounces of California mashed avocado on top and serve.

Gyro-Style Pork Sandwich (George Foreman Grill)

I use a George Foreman grill to make this very authentic-tasting Gyro, but you can also use the oven.

1 pound boneless pork loin 4 tablespoons olive oil

1 tablespoon prepared mustard 1 teaspoon ground cumin

1/3 cup lemon juice

3 cloves garlic, minced

1 teaspoon dried oregano 1 cup sour cream

cucumber, peeled, seeded, shredded and drained 1/2 teaspoon garlic, crushed

1/2 teaspoon dill

large pita loaves, halved (or 4 small ones) 1 small red onion, peeled and thinly sliced Lettuce and tomato slices

Cut pork crosswise into thin slices. Slice the into strips 5 x 1/2-inch.

Combine olive oil, mustard, cumin, lemon juice, minced garlic and oregano. Pour over pork slices. Cover and refrigerate for 1 to 8 hours.

Meanwhile, in small bowl stir together sour cream, cucumber, crushed garlic and dill. Cover and refrigerate.

If using the oven, preheat it to 450 degrees F. Drain marinade from pork slices and place pork in single layer in shallow pan. Roast until crisp, about 10 minutes.

If using the George Foreman grill (or similar), preheat the grill for 3 minutes. Drain the pork slices very well and place on the grill. Cook for six minutes, turning once. If your grill has the optional bun warmer, place the pitas in it to warm.

Open each pita to form a pocket. Distribute pork among each. Top each sandwich with some chilled cucumber mixture, sliced onions, lettuce and tomato slices.

Yield: 4 servings

Gyros

1 pound ground beef or lamb 2 tablespoons water

tablespoon lemon juice 1 teaspoon salt

1/2 teaspoon ground cumin

1/2 teaspoon dried oregano leaves 1/4 teaspoon pepper

cloves garlic, crushed 1 small onion, chopped

2 tablespoons vegetable oil

4 (6-inch diameter) pita breads 2 cups shredded lettuce

1/2 cup plain yogurt

1 tablespoon snipped fresh mint leaves or 1 teaspoon dried mint leaves

1 teaspoon granulated sugar

1 small cucumber, seeded and chopped 1 medium tomato, chopped

Mix beef or lamb, water, lemon juice, salt, cumin, oregano, pepper, garlic and onion. Shape into 4 thin patties. Cook patties in oil over medium heat, turning frequently, until done, about 10 to 12 minutes.

Split each pita bread halfway around edge with a sharp knife. Separate to form pocket. Place patty in each pocket; top with lettuce.

Mix yogurt, snipped mint and sugar; stir in cucumber. Spoon onto lettuce; top with tomato.

Hamburger Salad Sandwiches

1/4 pound hamburger

1 tablespoon chopped onion 1 cup shredded lettuce

1/2 cup shredded cheese 1 large dill pickle, chopped 1/2 cup mayonnaise

1 hardboiled egg, chopped (optional) 1 teaspoon salt

1/4 teaspoon pepper

Brown hamburger with salt and pepper. Drain and cool slightly. Add all other ingredients and stir well. Use for regular bread sandwiches or as a pita filling.

Hanky Panky

1 1/2 pounds lean ground beef 1 (12 ounce) package sausage

1 teaspoon Worcestershire sauce 8 ounces Velveeta cheese

Place ground beef and sausage in a large skillet. Cook over medium high heat until evenly brown. Drain the meat and mix in Worcestershire sauce. Spread cheese over meat, allowing it to melt.

Serve warm on slices of bread.

Harley Hog Sandwich

1 (6 to 8 pound) boneless pork butt, tied 12 large round rolls

Rub

1 cup kosher salt

cup coarsely-ground black pepper 1 cup sweet Hungarian paprika

cups hickory wood chips 1 cup apple wood chips

Combine kosher salt, black pepper and paprika. Coat pork butt evenly with mixture, shaking off any excess. Soak wood chips in water 30 minutes.

Place pork butt in smoker on rack at 220 degrees F for 8 hours, with smoke going for 2 hours. Let cool slightly. Break meat apart with hands.

Hog Sauce

large onions, chopped

tablespoons vegetable oil 1 tablespoon paprika

1 tablespoon chili powder

1 tablespoon red pepper flakes 1/2 teaspoon cayenne pepper 1/2 teaspoon ground cumin

42 ounces canned tomatoes with juice 3 cups cider vinegar

1 3/4 cups catsup 1/2 cup orange juice

1/2 cup dark brown sugar, packed 1/4 cup brown mustard

1 tablespoon salt

1 tablespoon cracked black pepper

Sauté onions in oil in heavy saucepan until translucent. Add spices and cook until fragrant. Add remaining ingredients and cook until mixture is thick and coats back of spoon. Purée sauce and let cool. (Sauce can be made 2 to 3 days in advance and refrigerated.)

Combine pork and sauce (to taste) in heavy saucepan. Cook until heated through. Pile pork on roll.

Serve with French fries and cole slaw, if desired.